Building Communities of Readers

continues over

Contents

Contents

UKLA

Building Communities of Readers - the project

1 Introduction and background

Recurring evidence suggests that children in England continue to read less independently and find less pleasure in reading than many of their peers in other countries (Twist, Schagen and Hodgson, 2003; 2007), so actively fostering positive attitudes to reading in the primary years has become crucial. The 2006 Progress in International Reading Literacy Study (PIRLS) also revealed that reading attainment in England has fallen significantly since the 2001 PIRLS (Twist *et al.*, 2007). The earlier PIRLS study, which involved comparing ten year olds in 35 countries, revealed that 13% of the English children disliked reading, compared to 6% on average (Mullis *et al.*, 2003; *et al.*, 2003). In the later study, which involved 41 countries, only 28% of the English children reported reading weekly compared to an international average of 40%. These results are in line with other studies which suggest a decline in children's reading for pleasure (e.g. OECD, 2001; Sainsbury and Schagen, 2004).

What primary children choose to read continues to change; outside school they read a diverse range of texts and report a preference for jokes, magazines, comics, fiction, TV books and magazines, poetry and websites in that order (Clark and Foster, 2005). Other studies also affirm that comics and magazines are popular (Maynard *et al.*, 2007) and that children prefer engaging with multimodal screen based texts (such as TV/DVD/ video/the internet) over those composed mainly of words (e.g. Nestlé Family Monitor, 2003; Bearne *et al.*, 2007) although this is not necessarily to the detriment of their involvement in written texts (Bearne *et al.*, 2007).

In relation to the use of children's literature in the classroom, in the last decade the practice of relying upon extracts has been heavily criticised (Dombey, 1998; Frater, 2000; Sedgwick, 2001) and professional writers too have voiced their concerns, arguing that an atmosphere of 'anxiety' exists around reading literature (Powling *et al.*, 2003, 2005). Many have suggested that if comprehension and assessment are seen to dominate over reading and response, this may adversely affect children's desire to read (King, 2001; Martin, 2003; Cremin, 2007). In addition, it has been noted that teachers' confidence in knowing and using children's literature may be limited (Arts Council England, 2003).

Studies of effective teachers of literacy show that teachers need much more than knowledge of phonic skills and comprehension strategies, they also need extensive knowledge of children's literature (Medwell *et al.*, 1998; Block, Oakar and Hurt, 2002). Yet such knowledge is not recognised as part of a primary teachers' professional repertoire in the new Standards for Teachers (TDA, 2007) in England, despite the fact that research from the US suggests continuity between teachers and children as engaged and self motivated readers (Morrison *et al.*, 1999; Bisplinghoff, 2003; Dreher, 2003; Commeyras *et al.*, 2003).

In response to this context, the United Kingdom Literacy Association undertook a study entitled *Teachers as Readers* 2006-7, which, drawing on questionnaires from 1200 primary teachers nationally, suggested that the majority are committed readers: three quarters had made time for their own independent reading within the last month. It also indicated that many of the teachers' own childhood favourites and poems that they were introduced to in school are still popular with them today and are used in their classrooms.

When asked to list 6 'good' children's writers, 64% of the teachers named five or six writers. 46% named six. Roald Dahl gained the highest number of mentions (744). The nearest four were: Michael Morpurgo (343), Jacqueline Wilson (323), J.K. Rowling (300) and Anne Fine (252).

When asked to name 6 good poets for children, 58% of the respondents named only one, two or no poet, 22% named no poets at all, only 10% named 6 poets. The highest number of mentions was for Michael Rosen (452) with five others gaining over a hundred mentions: Allan Ahlberg (207), Roger McGough (197), Roald Dahl (165), Spike Milligan (159) and Benjamin Zephaniah (131). With reference to picture fiction, over half the sample (62%) only named one, two or no picture fiction writers, 24% named no picture fiction authors/illustrators, whilst 10% named six. Many of these picturebook makers were also named as 'authors' in the first list. The highest number of mentions by far was for Quentin

Blake (423) with four others being mentioned over a hundred times: Anthony Browne (175), Shirley Hughes (123), Mick Inkpen (121) and Alan Alhberg (146). There were also 302 specifically named books rather than authors.

These findings raise the question of whether teachers are familiar with a sufficiently diverse range of writers to enable them to foster reader development and make informed recommendations to emerging readers with different needs and interests. The lack of professional knowledge and assurance with children's literature demonstrated and the minimal knowledge of global literature indicated has potentially serious consequences for learners. Furthermore, the infrequent mention of poetry in teachers' personal reading and their lack of knowledge of poets, as well as the relative absence of women poets and poets from other cultures writing in English is a concern, as is the dearth of knowledge of picture book creators, and the almost non-existent mention of picture book writers for older readers.

The evidence also brings into question the capacity of the profession to draw upon a wide enough range of children's authors in order to plan richly integrated and holistic literacy work and suggest that if units of work or author studies are undertaken, these are likely to be based around the work of writers from a limited canon of children's authors, whose writing may already be very well known to children. The wide popularity and teacher reliance on the prolific work of Dahl for example, may restrict children's reading repertoires, since child-based surveys suggest he is also a key author of choice for children.

Placed alongside the documented decline in reading for pleasure (Twist *et al.*, 2003, 2007) and the reduction in primary phase book spending (Hurd, 2006), the lack of teacher knowledge of children's literature evidenced in this research suggest a real need for increased professional attention and support in this area. Practitioners need ongoing opportunities to enrich their knowledge base and need to know how and where to access advice about books and writers. Local libraries and librarians are surely central to this, although evidence suggests they are not extensively drawn upon (Ofsted, 2004a; Cremin *et al.*, 2007).

Teachers' knowledge also deserves broadening in other ways, to encompass both the knowledge that develops through being a reader, and the rich pedagogical content knowledge that can support the development of independent, reflective and creative readers. Alongside gaining insights into their own practices and habits as readers, more emphasis is needed in this era of personalisation, on teachers working from children's own reading interests and preferences as they seek to introduce them to texts which motivate, build reading stamina and foster reader development.

Continuing professional development opportunities are urgently required to help teachers develop more diverse repertoires and to understand the value and role of literature in the growth of readers, so that they can foster, what Britton (1993) called, a potent 'legacy of past satisfactions'. Following the original phase of the UKLA research and development project *Teachers as Readers* (2006-2007), the second phase *Teachers as Readers: Building Communities of Readers* (2007-2008) offers just such a model for professional development.

2 Reflections on the project *Teachers as Readers: Building Communities of Readers*

The project *Teachers as Readers: Building Communities of Readers* was designed to develop children's independent reading for pleasure. This was undertaken in five local authorities in England: Barking and Dagenham, Birmingham, Kent, Medway, and Suffolk who worked within the given framework of the project and held local professional development sessions with their teachers. The fifty teachers involved also attended three national project meetings in London and case studied three children in their classes across the year.

The research and development project was externally evaluated (Durrant, 2008) and the research team collected and analysed data in relation to the research aims (Cremin *et al.*, 2008c). The project aimed to develop children's pleasure in reading, extend teachers' subject knowledge of children's literature, and their confident skilful use of such literature in the classroom. It also sought to develop teachers' relationships with parents, carers, librarians and families and create Reading Teachers: teachers who read and readers who teach.

The UKLA research team collected a wide range of data including:
- initial and final data encompassing children's perceptions surveys, and teachers' assessments of their focus children as well as teachers' questionnaires
- booktalk data gathered from the national meetings
- termly interviews and observations from the 10 case study schools, with headteachers, teachers and children
- ongoing data tracking the development of the three focus children per class, collected by the teachers
- ongoing reflective commentaries on the teachers' learning journeys as readers and as pedagogues.

Based on the early findings and initial observations, the team offer the following insights in relation to the aims and the value of action research to guide colleagues in schools, LAs and ITE institutions who wish to develop children's reading for pleasure.

Teachers' knowledge of children's literature

Through extensive reading aloud, book sharing, time for booktalk and focused discussion of texts, teachers widened their reading repertoire of children's authors. However, some teachers were initially reticent to engage with poetry or global literature for example and found reading 'outside their comfort zone' a challenge. The sustained support of the group and the local coordinator were significant in over-coming these difficulties. Negotiating specific self-set targets also worked well and offering teachers regular and committed time to share both their personal and professional reading in small groups appears to have been crucial. This helped build relationships, fostered a culture of book recommendations and reminded the teachers of reasons for reading, what influences their own choices and the pleasure to be found in reading and sharing literature.

Teachers' use of children's literature

Initially the majority of the teachers 'used' literature to plan units of work and as a resource to teach literacy skills. With a focus on children's independent reading for pleasure, gradually the teachers began to reinstate practices such as regular reading aloud, independent reading time and a wealth of book promotion/recommendation activities. However many found it hard to create the time to achieve this in a tightly timetabled curriculum and whilst convinced of the personal and social benefits of regular paired reading (between Year 5 and Year 2, for example) were less sure that this would influence attainment. Early indications suggest that providing increased time and focused support for independent reading influences both children's attainment and their attitudes to reading. In addition, reading aloud, book corners, reading promotion activities and building on children's own reading preferences and practices in the home were seen to be significant in influencing children's independent reading for pleasure. Such pedagogic practices widened both the teachers' and the children's conceptions of reading and enabled a better balance to be established between using literature for literacy instruction and supporting each child's development as a reader.

Teachers' relationships with parents, families and librarians

The teachers all sought to find out more about the diverse forms of reading undertaken in the home, and many established initiatives to involve parents, including sharing sessions in which parents enthused about their passions for reading about, for example, cake icing, fashion, gardening or football. In addition, various 'Families Read Together' workshops were run and 'A Cushion, A Cuddle and A Cool Read' - paired parent reading sessions - were established during the school day. However, in many schools the teachers initially concentrated on building communities of readers in their classrooms and across the school, and only after a year's work began to seek more parental and community involvement. This was in part an issue of time and in part an issue of prioritising the classroom reading community. Strong links were made by many teachers with local libraries and visits and new partnerships established, with some children visiting their local library en masse for the first time. Such relationships can be built upon in diverse ways.

Teachers as Reading Teachers

The notion of 'Reading Teachers': teachers who read and readers who teach (Commeyras *et al.* 2003), is a complex one. It involves teachers sharing their adult reading practices and preferences, their reading habits and histories with children in ways that prompt children to consider and share their own. Some teachers found this difficult initially as they were reticent to share their reading identities and unsure of the validity of this strategy, but gradually they grew in confidence and found it liberating and empowering both to themselves and the children. They found that focusing on books which they and the children had never finished, for example, or sharing the diversity of what they read, needed to be made very explicit in the classroom in order to explore and validate the children's rights as readers.

Action research

The teachers all undertook case studies of focus children. Through carefully collecting information, observing and documenting the impact of their changing pedagogy and practice, they became convinced of the value of the ongoing action research and collected evidence of the impact of their changed practice and subject knowledge on the children. Many used this data to convince colleagues, the senior management team, parents/ carers and governors that profiling reading for pleasure and widening their subject knowledge and classroom practice can make a significant contribution both to children's attitudes and attainment. The value of placing action research at the centre of this project should not be underestimated.

Collaborative partnerships

The project was developed collaboratively across five local authorities through regional co-coordinators who sought help from librarians, publishers, a children's literature consultant (Prue Goodwin) and a steering committee from the Qualifications and Curriculum Authority, the National Literacy Trust, OfSTED and the Schools Library Service. This helped build networks of contacts and offered real support. Regional co-ordinators and teachers valued the opportunity to work with others from different LAs. Other connections who can provide valuable literature expertise would include librarians, local university colleagues, publishers and/or independent consultants. Section 6 also provides useful websites.

3 Project principles and aims

This was an action research project. By the end of the project it was anticipated that the teachers should have understood the significance of reading for pleasure in the progression and development of young readers, and recognised their role as professionals in planning for and nurturing children's independent reading for pleasure.

Project principles

The project focused on building communities of readers within and beyond the classroom that would offer appropriate support and encouragement to children as readers and facilitate reader development. Ultimately, the project aimed to improve children's independent reading for pleasure.

Drawing on national and international research evidence, *Building Communities of Readers* was based on the following underpinning assertions:

a) that increasing children's independent reading for pleasure will lead to improved reading attainment
b) that increasing children's independent reading for pleasure contributes to children's lifelong positive reading habits
c) that children's independent reading for pleasure will be influenced by a number of factors outside school and a wealth of teacher-related factors inside school, including:
   i.   teachers' subject knowledge of a wide range of children's literature
   ii. teachers' confidence and skills in using children's literature with the aim of promoting reading for pleasure
   iii. teachers' abilities to build strong communities of engaged and interactive readers in classrooms and beyond the school with parents, carers and librarians
   iv. teachers' own reading habits and ability to share their reading lives with the children in order to support them as engaged readers (i.e. being Reading Teachers, teachers who read and readers who teach)
d) that teachers' reading knowledge, confidence, skills, and reflective practice can be enhanced through challenging yet supportive networks and new reading partnerships
e) that action research will assist teachers in enhancing their own practice and children's pleasure and achievements in reading.

Project aims

The teachers worked towards the following four aims, albeit giving more emphasis to some in their school development work than others, in response to identified school needs and priorities.

The project aimed to:
1) Widen teachers' knowledge of children's literature in order to support independent reading for pleasure.
2) Develop teachers' confidence and skilful use of such literature in the classroom in order to foster reading for pleasure.
3) Develop teachers' relationships with parents, carers, librarians and families, in order to support independent reading for pleasure.
4) Enable teachers to understand the value of becoming a Reading Teacher: a teacher who reads and a reader who teaches in order to support independent reading for pleasure.

Aim 1: Widen teachers' knowledge of children's literature in order to support independent reading for pleasure.

By the end of the project the teachers should have:

1 a) widened their knowledge of children's authors and contemporary writers
1 b) extended their knowledge of challenging picture fiction creators for key stage 1 or 2
1 c) widened their knowledge of children's poets, both contemporary and classic
1 d) extended their knowledge of children's comics and magazines.

Aim 2: Develop teachers' confidence and skilful use of such literature in the classroom in order to foster reading for pleasure.

By the end of the project the teachers should have:

2 a) planned, organised and sustained regular opportunities for children to read independently for for pleasure
2 b) found ways of sustaining regular reading aloud to the class for pleasure
2 c) planned, undertaken and sustained regular book promotion activities in school
2 d) made individual as well as whole class text recommendations, using their knowledge of the learners and of texts.

Aim 3: Develop teachers' relationships with parents, carers, librarians and families in order to support independent reading for pleasure.

By the end of the project the teachers should have:

3 a) discovered useful information about children's out-of-school reading habits, cultures and practices
3 b) formed understandings with families and communities about what it means to be 'a reader' in the 21st century
3 c) re-shaped classroom reading pedagogies in ways that value and build on children's out-of-school reading experiences
3 d) built sustained and mutually beneficial relationships between schools, families and local library services.

Aim 4: Develop Reading Teachers, teachers who read and readers who teach in order to support independent reading for pleasure.

By the end of this project the teachers should have:

4 a) reflected upon their own reading histories and current practices and explored the consequences for classroom practice
4 b) developed new ways of sharing their own reading preferences, processes and reading identities with the children
4 c) developed the children's rights as readers, demonstrating that readers can and do choose what, when and where to read.

The project was also aware that building capacity and developing sustainability are key issues which local authority co-ordinators and literacy consultants in schools would wish to address in order to facilitate a more permanent change in the reading culture and ethos of schools. In order to achieve this it was recommended that the project should be developed alongside more focused one-to-one approaches such as Every Child a Reader (ECaR) and teachers' assessment procedures such as Assessing Pupil Progress in Reading (APP).

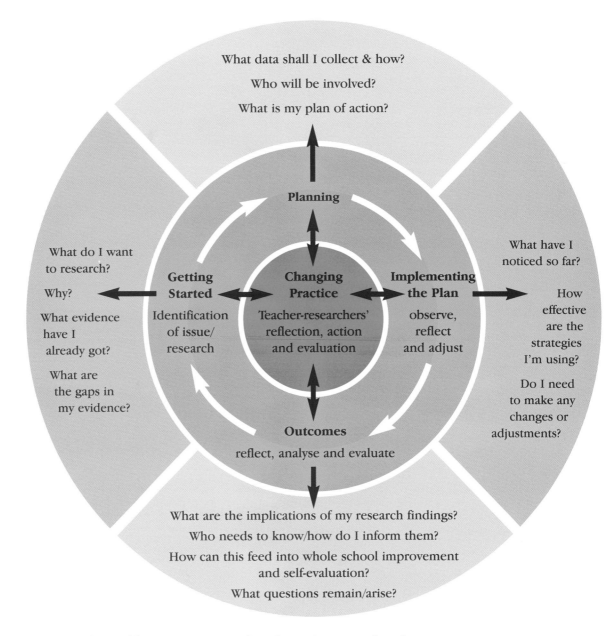

Figure 1 The *Building Communities of Readers* action research cycle

4 Framework for *Building a Community of Readers* project

The following section provides a framework for anyone who wishes to carry out a project similar to *Building Communities of Readers*. It gives details of how you might organise an action research project aimed at developing teachers' and children's experience and enjoyment of reading and suggests how the teachers involved might build a portfolio of evidence.

Action research

Before describing the details of the project, we include a brief overview of the underpinning principles of action research as well as some guidance about how to approach an action research project. An important proviso to bear in mind is that the focus, aims, design and implementation of such projects should be developed in collaboration with the teacher-researchers and should be appropriate to their contexts, albeit under the umbrella of one or more of the chosen aims of a *Building Communities of Readers* project.

Action research is one way of implementing change and introducing new ideas into classrooms and
schools based on evidence of what is currently happening in particular circumstances. It is a process by
which practitioners and schools initiate questions relating specifically to their particular contexts and
seek solutions by examining and assessing their own work and considering ways of working differently.

One of the advantages of action research is that it gives schools the opportunity to lead and manage
change for themselves. It involves collecting a range of evidence on which to base rigorous reflection
It is based on the following assumptions:

- Teachers and schools work best on issues they have identified for themselves.
- They need time and space to reflect on, evaluate and to experiment with practice in order to
  respond to the circumstances and needs of particular children, schools and communities.
- Teachers and schools can best help each other by working collaboratively.
- Action research involves collecting a range of evidence (qualitative and quantitative) from which
  to analyse strengths and weaknesses.
- Action research contributes to a culture of self evaluation and school improvement.

When teachers carry out an action research project it is likely that it will have an impact on others. Hitchcock
and Hughes describe the principal features of action research as '*change* (action) and *collaboration*
between researchers and researched' (1995:27). As such, it is important that the research is justifiable,
has clear aims and objectives, and stands up to ethical scrutiny (see below).

Action research is systematic and cyclical with reflective practice at the centre of that cycle. It also
involves interrelated, overarching strands of data collection and analysis.

- The first is an analysis of personal practice, how it links to theory (which may be implicit or explicit),
  and what effects it has on others. It also involves documenting changes over time as you become
  more aware of thought and action, and perhaps change your (and others') beliefs and / or actions.

- The second is an analysis of the context in which you work and the subject or issue you are interested
  in (including the people you work with) and the effects of your beliefs and practices on these (and
  the effects of your context and other people on you). The context is not just your school, but can
  include the bigger picture such as educational policies and social issues.

Figure 1 (shown left) represents the research cycle of the *Building Communities of Readers* project.
The inner boxes reflect the stages of the action research, which trigger ongoing reflection about personal
values, learning and interaction with the process, as well as ongoing review of the evidence which supports
and informs the process. The outer boxes indicate the questions which underpin each stage.

Research ethics

It is important to ensure that teachers attend to the ethic of respect and their responsibilities as
researchers as noted in the BERA (2004) Revised Ethical Guidelines for Educational Research. These are
freely available to download from: http://www.bera.ac.uk/publications/guides.php

If teacher-researchers intend to share any information gathered with others or across the authority, consent
must be obtained from those involved (Please see A5).

Researching others peoples' values, beliefs, understandings and behaviours is not a right, but a privilege,
and in order to engage in such collaborative reflection and ethical practice, it is helpful for teachers to
discuss what they are intending to do with all those involved, giving them meaningful information about
their aims and objectives. Sharing plans can also help raise the profile of the work and provoke interest.
Practically and also ethically there are legal issues to consider including child protection matters. If the
teachers want to take photographs, for example, or gather information that is different from what they
would normally expect to find out in the course of their work as teachers, they will need to obtain both
parents' and children's consent. Teachers may want to consider the following frequently asked questions

when thinking about the ethics of their research and the information:

- What is the project about?
- What is the justification for the project?
- What are the project aims?
- How will the research be conducted?
- What does being involved mean for different people?
- Can a participant opt out?
- Will there be any disadvantages?
- Will participants be anonymous?
- What will happen to the information?
- What will be the benefits of being involved?
- How and when will the findings be disseminated and to whom?

The project process

The project framework outlined here is based on a model of action research and therefore involves children and teachers learning together. Throughout the project, the teachers build a portfolio of evidence and reflection to support their research. Section Two includes all the proformas which support the process. Detailed guidance for each term and suggested sessions for achieving each of the project aims follows in this section but in brief, the process involves:

Pupil learning

Teachers select a small focus group of three pupils. They will need to make some close observations of these children's reading behaviours and competencies over the period of the project. They will also be asked to provide a range of data about these pupils at the beginning and end of the project. Proformas to support data gathering are provided in Section Two (A1 - A5).

Teachers are likely to use school data to identify the focus pupils. These should include those who can - but rarely choose to - read for pleasure. In the early years where such a distinction is less appropriate, it is recommended that children are selected who seem not to show any early reading behaviours or who may be unfamiliar with books. These learners would mostly be children who are less successful at literacy, pupils who are at risk of failure in literacy or who are making slow progress. They may be recent arrivals to the UK. Generally it is wise not to include children with severe special needs or statements.

Professional learning

Teachers document their own reading over the period of the project and note ways in which this contributes to classroom practice. Materials to support this are provided in Section Two (B1-B7).

Research question/focus area

The group of teachers involved may be working with one research question or individual teachers may generate their own questions with a particular school focus. Of course, these may be modified during the course of the project.

Dissemination

Teachers will need to draw their project together with a final presentation of their results. This presentation can be used for whole school dissemination or/and for sharing across clusters of schools within the local authority (see B6).

The grid in Figure 2 provides guidance for termly priorities. Pages 17 to 30 give detailed suggestions for sessions designed to achieve Aims 1-4.

Right **Figure 2** Termly priorities for the project process

Term	Main Focus
Autumn During this term the project coordinator will support the teachers with Aims 1, 2 and 3 in centre-based sessions (and maybe in other ways throughout the project). The coordinator should also establish a link with the library services to plan to support the work of the project. This will become more important in the spring term. Forms A1, A2, B1, B2 to be completed at the start of term, and A3, B3, B4 to be completed by the end of the term.	**Phase 1: Getting Started and Planning** • Extend teachers' subject knowledge of children's literature. (Aim 1) • Enhance teachers' confidence and skilful use of such literature in the classroom. (Aim 2) • Enable teachers to understand the value of becoming a Reading Teacher. (Aim 4) • *In this phase teachers will be gathering a range of start data from their focus pupils and their own professional learning.* • *With support, teachers will plan a programme of action to start at the end of the Autumn Term/early Spring Term and to address Aims 3 and 4.*
Spring As the project progresses, the teachers will be collecting evidence of any change in the focus pupils. They may need to adjust strategies and maybe even change direction to meet the needs of the young readers. Centre-based sessions will be an important opportunity for the teachers to spend time in critical reflection and peer discussions. Forms A3, B3 and B4 to be completed by the end of the term.	**Phase 2: Implementing the Plan.** • Continue to extend teachers' knowledge and use of literature. (Aims 1 and 2) • Develop clear links/relationships with parents, carers, librarians and families. (Aim 3) • Explore various strategies to enable teachers to develop as Reading Teachers. (Aim 4) • *In this phase teachers will be trying new strategies, reviewing and evaluating their effectiveness and sharing practice.* • *As the term progresses teachers will need to find appropriate, workable ways of documenting any evidence of impact on the pupils' reading behaviours and attitudes and any change in community relationships.*
Summer Towards the middle of the term the project coordinator will support the teachers as they gather their end-of-project data. The teachers may value support as they reflect upon, analyse and evaluate the impact of their project development work. Forms A1, A2, A3, A4, and B1, B3, B4, B5, B6 and B7 to be completed towards the end of the term.	**Phase 3: Continued Implementation and Examining Outcomes** • Continue to extend teachers' knowledge and use of literature, their relationships with parents, carers, librarians and families and their role as Reading Teachers. (Aims 1-4) • *In this final phase teachers will need to return to all parts of their baseline/start data and consider what impact the project has had on the focus pupils/on their own practice:* • *What key issues has this work raised?* • *What are the implications for further development?*

Data gathering

The teachers engaged in this project will need to collect two sources of data for their portfolios:
- data relating to their own professional learning journeys which will encompass evidence of links made between pupils, families, communities and libraries
- data relating to the learning journeys of their three focus children in class.

They will also need to:
- negotiate with all those involved in the project to develop comfortable ways of working
- consider ethical issues relevant to their situation (see p 11)
- discuss with their headteacher the school policy for seeking parental permission to photograph video or audiotape children
- seek written permission from parents to use their children's voices, images, writing or drawing (See sheet A5 Parent/ Carer Consent Guidance)
- identify three case-study children
- record information about school policy and documentation, their personal reading, notes, photographs and other information relevant to their personal projects (B5 p 45).

Teachers' professional learning

As the project progresses, teachers will be keeping records of their own journeys by:

- completing the Teachers' Questionnaire at the beginning and end of the project (B1 p 39)
- completing the Personal Reading History sheets at the beginning of the project (B2 p 41)
- completing a Termly Reflection on Being a Reading Teacher (B3 p 42)
- completing Termly Reflections on Impact (B4 p 44)
- presenting their development work to the rest of the group (B6 p 46)
- completing a Final Project Evaluation (B7 p 48).

Pupil data

This project aims to do much more than measure pupils' reading performance in terms of level descriptors. It is necessary, therefore, for the teachers to gather a range of information and data on the focus pupils, including attitudinal and behavioural aspects and self perception surveys:

- *before and after the project*, focus pupils complete the Children's Reading Survey (A1 p 33)
- *before and after the project*, teachers complete Children's Reading Profiles for each of their focus pupils (A2 p 35)
- *during the project*, teachers complete Termly Observations of Case Study Children (A3 p 36).

This data collection will help provide base-line information across the whole project. Although it is essential to keep data on the focus group children, teachers may want to complete the Children's Reading Survey with the whole class as it is likely to yield important information for planning intervention strategies.

As the project progresses teachers will make observational notes on each of their three focus pupils on the Termly Observations of Case Study Children form (A3). Some teachers may also wish to complete a research journal to document their wider reading and their observations of the children; these would be kept in their portfolios.

Autumn Term: Getting Started and Planning

In the teacher discussion and feedback sessions this term, facilitators will need to allow time for teachers to reflect on:

- their views of themselves as readers in the questionnaire and reading history (B1 and B2)
- their personal reading targets - teachers may wish to record/review these in some form

- what they have noticed from the children's reading surveys, reading profiles and observations (A1, A2, A3)
- their school plans for the project (B5)
- their reflections on being a Reading Teacher (B3)
- the overall impact of the project this term (B4).

Spring Term: Implementing the Plan

This term, in which they are implementing their plans and developing work in class and school, the emphasis in the discussion and feedback sessions will need to include time to:

- share the strategies/approaches being tried, adjusting plans as necessary
- complete and discuss the termly observations of the case study children (A3)
- collect additional child information about responses to the pedagogic changes (A4)
- reflect on being a Reading Teacher (B3)
- review the overall impact of the project this term (B4).

Summer Term: Continued Implementation and Examining Outcomes: reflection, analysis and evaluation

In this term the teachers continue to develop their work and move into the final critical evaluative phase in which they will share their findings with others. They will need time in discussion and feedback sessions to:

- complete the termly observations of the case study children (A3)
- reflect upon being a Reading Teacher (B3)
- review the overall impact of the project this term (B4)
- continue collecting additional child information about responses to the pedagogic changes (A4)
- continue collecting relevant additional information (B5)
- collect and analyse the children's reading surveys and reading profiles in order to compare end point data with the baseline/start data (A1 and A2)
- consider the overall impact of the project in the final presentation (B6) and evaluation (B7)
- identify key issues about practice and policy raised by their work.

Section Two includes an information sheet (Teacher Portfolio Support Materials p 32) which can be photocopied and given to each of the project teachers as a guide for their portfolios.

Ongoing review and evaluation

In centre-based sessions it will be important to give teachers time to reflect on the progress and impact of the project and complete the reflection proformas. Good project management includes recognising what the key research questions are and adopting appropriate methods to gather evidence, but it also involves asking questions about whether the research is progressing as planned and if the strategies or methods are achieving what the teachers were aiming for. Making the process transparent contributes to the reliability of the research and credibility of findings and conclusions.

Embedding the practice of reviewing and evaluating progress in the project and supporting the teachers collecting and analysing evidence of impact will help to ensure the project is on track. Without evidence you cannot substantiate any claims that the project has led to particular benefits or outcomes. If you hope to repeat the project or develop it with other schools, the process of reviewing and evaluating the project can help to provide you with reasons to continue (or not) and may support any applications for funding within or beyond your local context.

Section 1

Teachers will need to keep evidence of their development work and their reflection sheets as well as the children's data in their portfolios. These will form part of the evidence of the teachers' professional development and their journeys towards their school aims regarding developing children's reading for pleasure. You may also wish to analyse this evidence to ascertain patterns and trends across the group as a whole.

Planning for change (Figure 3) can help you as project co-ordinator to review and evaluate the project on a continuous basis via regular communications and meetings. It follows the process of planning and carrying out a project. If used, the objectives should be developed in collaboration with the teacher-researchers involved in the project and the resources negotiated with them. A chart like this can help to clarify aims and methods in the project's early stages and to review progress and milestones later on. It is a useful tool for considering whether appropriate actions and methods are being undertaken and what evidence is being generated.

Aim	Objectives	Resources needed/inputs	Activities	Intended Outcomes Short Term	Intended Outcomes Longer Term
Negotiate, agree and insert your overarching aim for the project. (Your intended outcomes should be linked to this aim). For example: *to increase children's reading for pleasure*	For example: *to increase teachers' subject knowledge of poetry; to make closer links with local library; to develop children's independent reading*	For example: *LA time; teacher time; expert input; materials loaned from library; texts drawn from the community*	For example: *LA conference for head-teachers; CPD sessions on teachers' own reading; visits to local library; strategies to develop 'read-aloud' across the school; inviting parents to participate in reading sessions*	For example: *teachers' subject knowledge of poetry increases; closer links developed with local library; children show greater engagement with reading*	For example: *increased levels of motivation and enthusiasm for reading across the school; established reading partnerships between home, school and community; broader range of reading materials used linking home and school preferences; raised levels of attainment in reading*

Figure 3 Planning for Change

5 Implementing the project aims

This section gives suggestions for professional development sessions (afternoons or staff meetings) designed to achieve the four aims of the project. According to your chosen focus, you may wish to select particular sessions, however, in addition you will need to allocate time for:

- sharing the data being collected about the children in the initial audit and throughout the project
- completing the various surveys and reflection sheets detailed in the teacher portfolio support materials in Section Two.

You are likely to want to focus on Aims 1 and 2, and begin to address Aim 4, during the first term of the work and plan to extend the work to Aim 3 and continue with Aims1, 2 and 4 during the second and third terms.

You may want to run a launch meeting, or allow time at the beginning of the first meeting, for the teachers to complete the Teachers as Readers questionnaire (B1). If the questionnaire is completed before the next session you will have time to summarise the information to feed back to the group. A launch meeting like this will may also be a time to share books from a book box established by a link with the library service.

Aim 1: Widen teachers' knowledge of children's literature in order to support independent reading for pleasure.

1 a) Widening knowledge of children's authors and contemporary writers

This session is designed to help teachers identify their own targets to extend their personal reading of children's books.

Before the session:
Invite teachers to bring in some of their (favourite) childhood books. Ask teachers to complete the Teachers as Readers questionnaire (B1).

During the session:
Share the teachers' favourite books informally, discussing their personal significance and asking them to identify why they chose them. Do they still use them in school?

Outline some of the findings from the UKLA *Teachers as Readers Phase 1* project, particularly the evidence which suggests that teachers are committed readers and read a wide range, including popular fiction (40%), thrillers (15%)) and crime stories (9%). You may want to stress that professionally the teachers in the research tended to rely on old childhood favourites and a limited canon of well known authors, and had particularly limited poetry and picture fiction repertoires. (See Recommended Reading (page 31) Cremin *et al.*, 2008) or access the PowerPoint™ of the findings at www/ukla.org). As there is a lot of information here, you may want to print off copies of the research report for the teachers in the group.

In the session, you might focus on the following:
In considering their ability to name six children's authors, poets and picturebook makers, it is questionable whether [the teachers] know a sufficiently diverse range of writers to enable them to foster reader development and make informed recommendations to emerging readers with different needs and interests. (Cremin, Mottram, Bearne and Goodwin, 2008b).

The choice of books and teachers' mediation of them has a profound effect on 'how (children) see themselves and who they want to be' (McCarthey and Moje, 2002:148).

Discuss these issues, presenting the findings from the group's responses to the teachers' questionnaire (B1). The findings from the original research and the teachers' own questionnaire responses should support the development of a fairly robust challenge to the teachers to identify individual or group targets for personal reading of children's texts.

The teachers can read at home and in school during independent reading and should review their targets and set new ones at the start of each term. Agree a first challenge with teachers, perhaps selecting from your book box established by the library link or from books you have supplied, and/or agree a core book/author focus for everyone to undertake by next time. Suggest the group ask their children for recommendations and that together you will construct a booklist to support others by the end of the year.

> *Knowing more authors has made the world of difference to my teaching, I recommend books now to particular children and have begun to plan more of my own work using writers I never knew existed before.* (Teacher, Suffolk).

1 b) Extending knowledge of challenging picture fiction creators for KS1/ 2

This session aims not only to help teachers extend their knowledge of picturebook fiction, but to encourage them to plan and carry out units of work based on challenging picturebooks.

Before the session:
Ask the teachers to bring three books by one of their favourite picture fiction creators. Share these in small groups. Select a few books by the same picturebook maker as a basis for discussing author studies.

During the session:
Using a high quality challenging picturebook partly imported into the IWB, share and discuss it together:

- how do the images complement or contradict the written text?
- what other texts does this remind the group of?
- what puzzles the readers?

You may want to consider authorial intentions, moral ideas, artistic styles and conventions and more. After engaging with the text's meaning, which might include drawing, drama or storytelling as one of the characters, involve the teachers in planning activities from this text for an extended unit of work.

Texts popular with a wide range of ages include for example *The Snow Dragon* by Vivian French, *Little Mouse's Big Book of Fears* or *Meerkat Mail* by Emily Gravett. For other ideas see the website list in Recommended Reading (p 31).

Show the teachers several other books by the same author and make it clear that reading aloud from the same writer and offering an author collection, setting up a literature circle or creating an author's display table with books, photographs, interviews and downloadable material etc. can be very valuable to enable the children to become better acquainted with different writers. It will also be important to offer time to talk about the stories in depth, making life-to-text and text-to-life connections, just as the teachers will have done with the book you shared.

> *My children now check out the names of authors and illustrators before choosing a book. Before they just grabbed the nearest one – now they're more discerning.* (Teacher, Barking and Dagenham)

Challenge the teachers to find a picture book author new to them and bring to the next session as many books as possible by this author, having worked on one of their stories and used the others in various ways. They will need to seek out information about the picture book author and come prepared to profile this writer, perhaps in a PowerPoint™ for the rest of the group. Such an activity could be repeated in later sessions as their knowledge about different writers expands.

We have emphasised... our delight in the children's intellectual excitement at analysing visual texts and how it deepened over time and exposure to picture books which they were engaged with emotionally and aesthetically. This brings us back to what we consider to be the 'basics' - the power of literature (visual and verbal) to move, enthral, and enrich our lives.
(Arizpe and Styles, 2003:248)

1 c) Widening knowledge of children's poets, both contemporary and classic

This session is designed to explore and enjoy a range of poetry and to plan to include more poetry reading in the school day and week.

Before the session:
Create a poetry box. You may want to borrow from the library a collection of children's poetry books and tapes, seeking out single author collections and work by contemporary writers, or invite a local librarian with knowledge of children's poets to join you for the session.

During the session:
Read aloud a few of your favourites and invite the teachers to recall some of their favourite poets or poems which they read in class and to browse the books and share informally.

Share with the teachers the recent Ofsted (2007) findings that primary professionals tend to lean on classic poetry and particular named poems and often select easy poetry for imitative writing purposes. Additionally, the UKLA *Teachers as Readers* research revealed that 58% of the 1200 primary respondents named only two, one or no poets, 22% named no poets at all and only 10% named six poets (Cremin *et al.*, 2007). Consider with the teachers why they think poets are not well known and the consequences of this.

Invite the teachers to borrow from the poetry box, read personally, share some in class and return next session with activities, ideas and accounts of the opportunities seized to bring poetry and poets to life. Classroom activities which the group might also undertake could include:

- visiting www.poetryarchive.org and in the children's archive listening to poets reading their work aloud
- making poetry posters in pairs; the children could choose 6-8 poems to include with at least one of their own
- creating group dances to self chosen poems from a read-aloud range
- establishing a regular poetry time and letting the children read, share, chat and find new poems form the classroom collection
- creating visual representations - murals, sculpture and drawing
- experimenting with performances, adding percussion, ostinatos, clapping, acting or PowerPoint™ backdrops.

It's only through listening to word in print being spoken that one discovers their colour, their life, their movement and drama. (Chambers, 1995:127)

Less experienced readers often find poetry offers immediate satisfaction and humorous poetry appeals to their sense of fun, but by bringing poetry to life they can also find pleasure in more complex verse. Pleasure and involvement precedes full understanding and it is possible to read aloud both immediately accessible and more complex verse in brief moments during the day.

When she reads some poems she slows down and kind of does actions and descriptions with them, so it's like... real. When the people turned into stone she kind of made it slow and we could see them turning into stone and it was brilliant - I love her reading poetry aloud. (Toby, aged 6)

1 d) Extending knowledge of children's comics and magazines

Comics and magazines aren't often part of the reading repertoire. This session opens up possibilities for teachers to include more graphic texts.

Before the session:
Purchase a selection of contemporary comics and magazines for primary aged readers, or invite the teachers to bring in a couple each as well as any magazines they often read.

During the session:
Start by focusing on their reading of these texts, both currently and in the past:
- what purposes did/does such reading serve for them as children/adults?

Take some time to read, enjoy and engage with the children's contemporary comics and magazines, perhaps in pairs identifying articles of interest, amusing cartoons and other features.

Discuss with the group the degree to which such popular literature is available for children to read in school. What implicit messages are conveyed by the professional use (or lack of it) of these texts? What value does such reading have?

> *I have no doubt of the significant part that comics played in my own and my daughter's development as both readers and writers... She has learned how to read 'writerly' text, understands a variety of uses of intertextuality, knows how cartoons can be used to persuade, inform and entertain. Perhaps most of all she has learnt some of the greatest pleasures that can come from sustained re-readings... Comics command reader identification and involvement.*
> (Bromley, 2000:42)

Make a list of the comics and magazines brought to the session and invite the teachers to become much better acquainted with a couple of these before the next session, when in role they can work as sales agents seeking to persuade reluctant newsagents to stock them. Also share possible strategies for ensuring children have access to such literature in class and recognise this as normal reading. These might include:

- creating comic/magazine surveys - which are the most widely read?
- teachers sharing in class memories of their favourite childhood comics/magazines
- establishing comic and magazine boxes and encouraging children to bring in their current comics/magazines for ERIC time
- focusing on comic characters though the use of TV and printed text, e.g. Minnie the Minx or Dennis the Menace, Bart Simpson
- focusing on comic and magazine titles - it's all in a name!
- creating a class magazine about issues that matter to the children
- using instructional texts from comics/magazines for teaching.

> *I'm going to take this Simpsons magazine to my desert island because I never ever get bored reading it and can read it again and again and again - they make me laugh.* (Callum, aged 10)

Aim 2: Develop teachers' confidence and skilful use of children's literature in the classroom in order to foster reading for pleasure.

2 a) Planning, organising and sustaining regular opportunities for children to read independently for pleasure.

This session is intended to encourage discussion about children's independent reading in the school and classroom. The teachers should consider the reading corners in their own classrooms and plan to develop them.

> *I know this is going to sound sad but I really like our reading homework.* (Danny, aged 11)

During the session:
Introduce the session by exploring some of the following questions in relation to the teachers' current practice:

- When do children have opportunities to read independently for pleasure?
- What has happened to ERIC (everyone reading in class) or USSR (uninterrupted sustained silent reading)?
- How should we organise ERIC or USSR so that it is meaningful for the children?
- Where can children read independently in the classroom?
- Where can children read independently in the school?
- Should independent reading always be silent?

You might then use the following comments from different teachers to stimulate the discussion further:

> *My children didn't seem to know what reading for pleasure is...*
> *The reading corner became the focal part of the classroom.*
> *There's a real culture in the class about reading.*
> *The biggest pluses are that my children are talking about books – both boys and girls.*
> (Teachers, Barking and Dagenham)

Invite the teachers to write a new section of the school policy on children reading independently for pleasure in school. Ask them to put together briefly what would go into this section, including their aims, where and when independent reading might occur, both in the classroom and across the school, and then discuss how they might monitor and evaluate this section of the policy.

> *I've got this cupboard in my room which is really big, and I've got a light inside... I sit in there... I put the light on and read in there... I sit on teddies and things.* (Nathan, aged 10)

The reading corner is the equivalent of Nathan's cupboard and needs to be a central part of the classroom. It is a space where a range of books, comics and other texts can be attractively displayed to entice the children into reading. Here the children can read quietly or share books with each other. Ask the groups to highlight what needs to be considered when designing a Reading Corner. The discussion might be stimulated through a selection of images on a Power Point™.

2 b) Finding ways of sustaining regular reading aloud to the class for pleasure

After this session the teachers might challenge themselves to make time for the pleasures (for both teacher and pupils) of reading aloud regularly.

My teacher read The Devil and His Boy *by Anthony Horowitz, it was really exciting.* (Jenny, aged 9)

Before the session:
Select a range of books which do and don't read aloud well, for each of the age groups represented by the group.

During the session:
Reading aloud is a routine which is now acknowledged to be significant in developing children as readers. Children are active meaning makers who make personal responses to texts as they connect readings to their own experiences and to a wide variety of other texts - (tele)visual, printed and oral - that they have encountered. As an introduction place the following statements on each of the tables and ask each group to discuss them:

High-quality reading-aloud sessions are the result of careful planning. (Washtell 2008: 72)

Listening to an expressive reading of a text helps young readers to understand how written language can be brought to life. (Barrs and Cork, 2001: 38)

When someone reads aloud, they raise you to the level of the book. They give you reading as a gift. (Pennac, 1994: 121)

From this point ask the groups to identify what else reading aloud gives to children. For instance:

- teacher modelling of reading
- common knowledge between all
- involving everyone
- introduction to new language and vocabulary in context
- opportunities to talk about story, situations, characters etc
- introduction to new texts, authors and genres.

In age phase groups give out a selection of books which do and don't read aloud well and ask the teachers to decide which is likely to read aloud well and why. From this point ask each group to draw up guidelines for staff on how to choose books to read aloud. Consideration needs to be given to: pace, action, length of chapters, vocabulary and repetition, and children's preferences and interests. To conclude, each group might draw up a list of books that they feel read aloud well, for example, *Six Dinner Sid* by Inga Moore or *The Firework Maker's Daughter* by Philip Pullman.

2 c) Planning, undertaking and sustaining regular book promotion activities in school

The original research showed that teachers are committed readers. This session aims to build on enthusiasm and encourage them to be advocates for children's books.

I realise that I have a massive influence on my children. If I'm enthusiastic they will be as well. (Teacher, Medway)

Teachers' influence in introducing pupils to new texts and authors was significant. (OfSTED, 2004b: 12)

Before the session:
Select a range of books for reading aloud to children for the group to share and discuss. You may want to find books that the teachers are unlikely to know. It would be useful if you had more than one copy of the book.
Find a variety of book covers, some of which are appealing and inviting and some which don't encourage you to open the book.

During the session:
Carry out a circle time with the teachers and ask each to talk about a recent children's book they have read and why they felt it was significant to them. Encourage them to discuss their responses to the story, the issues that arise and the questions that develop from the narrative. At the end of the activity ask them in pairs to explore how this activity could be used to promote books in a primary classroom.

When a group of *Building Communities of Readers* children were asked if they like their teacher suggesting books to them, they all responded positively, one said:

> Cos it helps you know like get your head around a book cos… you… she talks about books but you don't necessarily know but if she suggests them, and you might like some. (Liam, aged 8)

Discuss with the group what his teacher might have been doing to promote books in class.

Reading aloud is an excellent way of informing children about new and different authors and texts. On each table place a book that could be read aloud to children and ask the teachers to discuss different ways of encouraging the children to read this and other related books. What else can they add to the following list?

- display based on an author/theme and related books to be borrowed
- copies of the book to be borrowed with post-it reviews inside
- display of author's other books or thematically related texts
- author's website identified
- link to an adapted version of the book (if there is one).

In groups brainstorm how they, as readers, choose what they read. Themes might include: friends' recommendations, prize reviews, knowledge of writer, seeing the film. Children are no different, except that book covers seem to play a large part in their choice, also the way books are displayed in the classroom. Show the teachers a range of book covers - some which appeal and some that don't. A recent survey found that 22% of KS2 respondents often or very often chose books by the cover while 64% said they did sometimes. (Maynard *et al.*, 2007).

> *I always look at the front cover and then read the blurb.* (Amy, aged 10)

2 d) Making individual as well as whole class text recommendations using their knowledge of the learners and of texts

This session is designed to bring together the teachers' knowledge of their class as readers and their own developing knowledge of texts for children.

Before the session:
Ask the teachers to bring notes from a discussion with a particular child in their class about their reading, reading habits and personal interests.

You might select some of the following books or other series: *The Young James Bond* series by Charlie Higson, Dick King Smith's books, *Lola and Charlie* series by Lauren Child, *Horrid Henry* series by Francesca Simon, *This is the Bear* series by Sarah Hayes and *Wolf Brother* series by Michelle Paver.

During the session:

Knowing what children like to read, the type of readers they are and their out-school interests is a significant part of a teacher's role in developing children as readers. With this knowledge teachers can build on children's interests, habits and preferences.

> *Almost all pupils in the most effective schools had some freedom to choose their own books, graded at appropriate reading levels. Their choices were usually monitored by teachers who suggested new books and authors as a means of broadening their reading.* (Ofsted 2004b:13)

Talk to the group about how children develop in their choice of texts and books. You might cover areas such as:

- the developmental aspect of children's choice of books
- what they enjoy reading out of school
- re-reading and what it offers the reader
- how books help children grow emotionally, culturally and linguistically
- series reading.

Invite the teachers in groups to discuss their case-study children and make suggestions about what they each like to read, what they would suggest to these children and what else they would like to find out about them as readers. Ask them to design a framework of questions for a reading conference with any child which would help them explore their interests and reading practices at home, their favourite kinds of reading/authors and what they would like to read in the future.

Using the selection of series books, ask the teachers to match the following children with any of the list, suggesting more of their own that might also suit these learners:

- Year 4 boy - likes humour, series books, struggles with reading
- Year 5 boy - has read much of Anthony Horowitz, likes action, has stamina
- Year 6 girl - enjoys historical novels, has stamina, good reader
- Year 2 boy - likes animals and humour, reading chapter books
- Year 1 girl - likes reality, doesn't read much, needs pictures.

Aim 3: Develop teachers' relationships with parents, carers, librarians and families in order to support independent reading for pleasure.

3 a) Discovering useful information about children's out-of-school reading habits, cultures and practices

This session aims to encourage the teachers to consider how they might find out more about children's out-of-school reading in ways that include parents, families and communities.

Before the session:

If you think there will be time for the teachers to complete their own 'Rivers of Reading' (see below) make up a bag with all the reading you have done over the weekend, including recipes, labels, magazines, junk mail…

During the session:

Share with teachers some of the findings from the National Literacy Trust research: *An investigation into young people's self-perceptions as readers: An investigation including family, school and peer influences* (www.literacytrust.org.uk). This reveals that the top five most popular out-of-school reading materials are: magazines, websites, emails, blogs, networking chatrooms followed by fiction books, newspapers, and comics/graphic novels. Discuss what teachers currently know about their children's out-of-school reading preferences and habits, encouraging them to consider both paper-based and on-screen reading.

> *Children now have available to them many forms of text which include sound, voices, intonation, stance, gesture, movement, as well as print and image. These texts have changed the ways in which young readers expect to read, the ways they think and the ways they construct meaning.*
> (Bearne, 2003: 129)

There is no doubt that children are surrounded by and use a rich variety of multi-dimensional texts for leisure reading but it is clear that this is not in opposition to more traditional paper-based materials. The old and the new are complementary. Children who enjoy computer games read 'cheat' magazines to help them play better, and often the computer games are linked to popular television series, comics and magazines and books. What is clear is that children's out-of-school reading practices are inextricably linked to the wider social, cultural and historical contexts of their lives.

A good way to discover more about children's out-of-school reading is to invite children and their families to create a 'River' of all the reading they engage with over one weekend. Provide children with the outline of a River drawn onto an A3 sheet of paper with the instructions:

- Draw, stick on/write about anything you read over the weekend… comics, magazines, football programmes, books, television pages, DVD cases, computer games, cereal boxes, chocolate bars… anything and everything!
- Invite mum/dad/brothers/sisters/nan/granddad (anyone who fancies having a go) to add their own reading and write their name next to their bit.
- Bring it to school so that you can share all the reading you have done.

As an example for the children, the teachers may want to share their own reading over a weekend - magazines, recipes, labels as well as more familiar reading material - before they invite the children to do their own. If there were time, you might want to demonstrate this yourself, and invite the teachers to make their own rivers before the next session.

Other activities might include:

- inviting children and families to create 'book bags' of all their weekend reading to bring into school and share
- encouraging children and families to take photographs of all their reading activities across one week/end
- engaging the children as researchers - finding out about all the different reading activities in their homes and communities.

> *We read loads Miss don't we?* (Sean, aged 6)

3 b) Forming understandings with families and communities about what it means to be a reader in the 21st century

This session builds on the teachers' growing awareness of the extent and diversity of the children's out of school reading.

During the session:
Once the teachers are more aware of the diverse and broad repertoire of out of school reading activities that are relevant to children's everyday lives, invite them to discuss their understanding of what it means to be 'a reader' today. Situating reading in the context of the technological and culturally diverse world of the twenty-first century gives us the opportunity to go back to basics. It opens new opportunities for establishing understandings with families about what the term *reading for pleasure* means for young readers and can help to build bridges between community and school and between parent and teacher.

The approach encourages teachers to look for ways of drawing on the 'funds of knowledge' to be found in the informal literacy practices found in children's lives and in their homes and communities (Gonzalez and Moll, 2002). Ask teachers to discuss ways of using their knowledge of children's reading repertoires to make connections with parents/carers and open discussions about children's reading which go beyond the formal exchange about reading competencies.

> *I hadn't really thought about sharing magazines with her before... I hadn't thought about that as connected to something at school - like reading.* (Parent, Birmingham)
>
> *I didn't really think that when he was on the computer he was still reading.* (Parent, Medway)

Suggest that the teachers might invite their KS2 children to interview their family members about their memories of childhood reading. Agree questions and ways of recording (digi blue cameras, hand-held Disgo camcorders, MP3, note taking, Dictaphones). You might use the following quotes from parents to stimulate discussion about how reading is linked to historical, social and cultural contexts:

> *My mom got me into reading when I was about 17 and unemployed. She realised I was stuffed and she knew I liked football and... she got me into reading through that.* (Parent, Birmingham)
>
> *I remember I would love to read Islamic books and also I loved to read the history of many things.* (Parent, Birmingham school)

Share possible ways of finding out more about children's existing funds of knowledge concerning new ways of reading. You might want to use the survey proformas provided by the UKLA research *Reading on Screen* (Bearne *et al.*, 2007). The group might want to try:

- inviting children, parents and teachers to survey home experiences of digital technology at home and school
- inviting children to complete a survey of multimodal texts in the home (younger children will need support from families)
- inviting children to express their preferences
- completing Personal Reading Profiles - this can be based on a week's reading at home and at school - in literacy and across the curriculum.

3 c) Re-shaping classroom reading pedagogies in ways that value and build on children's out-of-school reading experiences

In this session the teachers have the chance to develop activities to promote talking about the children's out of school reading.

> *Talk about texts is one of the key ways in which readership networks are established. It is through talk about texts that what it means to read and to be a reader are jointly negotiated.* (Maybin and Moss, 1993: 139)

During the session:
Sensitive and reflective teachers know that there is a fine line between valuing and building on children's reading interests and choices and intruding into their worlds. It is important to discuss this with the teachers so that the 'sharing' of reading experiences in the classroom becomes a reciprocal process between children and teachers and an ethos of trust is established. You might want to discuss the quotation from Maybin and Moss with the teachers. The opportunity to talk with others about what you are reading and your reading practices at home is a crucial part of developing engaged and motivated readers. When does this happen in class?

Encourage the teachers to conduct a survey of their classroom reading environment:

- How are reading conversations encouraged?
- Are there special spaces for the children to read/share reading?
- Are there special spaces in the timetable?
- Considering what teachers now know about children's tastes and interests, is there an appropriate range of reading materials available?
- Are children encouraged to bring their own reading material into school?

> *I recommend this book to Kaseem because there are lots of jokes and quizzes in it and that's what he likes.* (Daniel aged 11)

There may be more reading going on in classrooms than teachers think. Encourage teachers to consider reading across the curriculum: multimodal, digital and print-based. They might list the different kinds of reading that they have engaged with in the last week - other than in literacy sessions. How much of this has been on-screen? interactive? moving image?

- What do teachers know about the expertise that children have in on-screen reading practices?
- How is this reflected in the classroom?

> *Online reading involves new texts which offer new challenges for teaching, for example, interactive texts and documentary video texts which appear on interactive websites... the structure of these texts involves different reading choices... teaching critical reading skills is vital.* (Bearne et al., 2007)

3 d) Building sustained and mutually beneficial relationships between schools, families and local library services

This session is important in identifying the extent to which teachers use library services.

Before the session:
Compile a brief survey to find out about the teachers' use of library facilities (see below).

During the session:
Phase 1 of the UKLA project, *Teachers as Readers*, identified that of 1,200 teachers across eleven local authorities in England, just 52 per cent of respondents use the local library facilities. There are demographic issues to consider, but the research showed a very strong correlation between using the local library for school and the local authority. This suggests that library provision not only varies but that, in some authorities, it is encouraged perhaps by literacy consultants and advisers as well as by historically strong links. A starting point for teachers may be a simple questionnaire to open discussion:

- Do you use your local library
  - for your own reading?
  - for your children's reading?
  - for your school?
- What does it provide?
- Do you use your schools' library service?
- Do you have a library within your own school?

Encourage teachers to contact or visit the local library to talk about ways of bringing together teachers, children, families and libraries to enrich and extend reading for pleasure and book-talk. Talk about how they might find ways of taking the class to the local library if this is not already happening.

> *Our local library is shut so we planned two visits to the nearest one. The bus journey was exciting for the children too because it took them out of the local area.* (Teacher, Birmingham)
>
> *Parents have been coming in and saying that the children are asking to go to the library.* (Teacher, Suffolk)

In discussions like this, teachers often identify the problems about using libraries. Encourage teachers to think of ways around barriers to library visits. It may be that electronic links can be established between the library and school for 'booktalk' conversations with librarians or perhaps librarians can visit the school.

> *We believe the link with the library is starting to build patterns for life with many of our children and parents. This summer's reading challenge has already taken on a whole new dimension.* (Headteacher, Kent)
>
> *Two of our Year 6 more challenging boys went missing after school one day. Search parties were just about to start out when they turned up. They had decided to drop into the library on their way home! We couldn't believe it!* (Headteacher, Suffolk)

Aim 4: Develop Reading Teachers, teachers who read and readers who teach in order to support independent reading for pleasure.

4 a) Reflecting upon personal reading histories and current practices and exploring the consequences for classroom practice

This session may well be one of the earliest sessions in the first term as a starting point for discussing what it means to be a Reading Teacher. Reading Teachers can be described as teachers who read and readers who teach (Commeyras *et al.*, 2003). Such teachers seek to apprentice younger readers and model their own love of reading in various ways, but all commit time to talk about their reading practices and then trigger space for children to talk about theirs. This can be mapped in as a regular feature of independent reading time.

Before the session:
Prepare personal reading History grids for the group (see p 41)

During the session:
In order for the teachers to consider their own reading histories and become more aware of the significant texts, people and places which influenced their views of reading, offer them time to record their responses to the themes below and then talk about memories of reading in childhood.

Personal Reading History		
Texts	**Significant People / Places**	**Talk**
Note all the kinds of reading you remember from when you were young: books, comics, magazines, newspapers, letters diaries, screen reading, maps, holy texts, songs, cereal boxes…	Was anyone involved in this reading with you? Where did you usually read?	What kinds of talk and conversations were involved?

> *'I can always tell when you're reading somewhere in this house' my mother used to say. 'There is a special silence, a reading silence'. I never heard it, this extra degree of hush that somehow travelled through the walls and ceilings to announce that my seven year old self had become about as absent as a present person could be.* (Spufford, 2002:1)

Invite the teachers to consider ways to enable the children to create their own reading histories. These might include:

- sending a similar/adapted sheet home as homework over a weekend
- visiting a classroom with books for younger readers, gathering a huge pile and returning to re-read, remember and enjoy, which should prompt memories of their early reading
- inviting the children to make a poster of their early memories with a photo of themselves in the centre
- sending children home in turns with a digi blue camera to interview their siblings, parents or grandparents about their early memories of reading. The teachers would need to agree appropriate questions with the children first.

> *It was great when we read those books again- I remembered so many of them, you knew what was coming, yet you still wanted to read on. I just LOVED it and I'm going to read some to my little sister.* (Elan, aged 10)

4 b) Developing new ways of sharing their own reading preferences, processes and reading identities with the children

This session is closely related to the previous one, aiming to prompt awareness that pupils' pleasure in reading is nurtured when teachers' lives and classroom practices are strongly influenced by their pleasure in literature:

> *Teachers who are engaged readers are motivated to read, are both strategic and knowledgeable readers, and are socially interactive about what they read. These qualities show up in their classroom interactions and help create students who are in turn engaged readers.* (Dreher, 2003:338)

Before the session:
Invite the teachers to record and collect what they read over 24/48 hours or undertake Rivers of Reading as a group (see Aim 3a p 24).

During the session:
In sharing something of themselves as readers who read a diverse range of texts (magazines, popular fiction, travel articles, newspapers etc), the teachers can identify intrinsic/extrinsic reasons for reading these. Challenge them to set up 24-hour reads in school where children can take photos of their reading matter and/or bring in samples to make posters and discuss their reading practices. Displays in entrance halls can be an effective way of conveying this reading diversity.

Activities which reflect being a Reading Teacher deserve to be mapped into practice. Discuss the following ideas, asking the teachers how they could they plan to ensure that such activities prompt the children to share their views. What else might they plan to include?

- sharing response to news items, with a newsboard and ongoing cut-outs
- sharing feelings about a passage, character or event in a text
- focusing on re-reading and what you have never chosen to read again
- discussing what gets in the way of reading for pleasure/leisure
- discussing reading habits e.g. skipping passages, reading the end before the end etc.
- developing Desert Island Choices of 4 key texts and connected displays.

> *Being a Reading Teacher makes me feel more connected to the children, we seem to have more in common now. Through sharing my reading life, I share more of my own views and values with them and they've opened up too. They're always talking about their reading, recommending books to me now or asking if I've read about certain things in the press.* (Teacher, Kent)

In seeking to build genuinely reciprocal reading relationships with children about reading, the teachers will be supporting the young readers' entitlement to be readers for life.

4 c) Developing the children's rights as readers, demonstrating that readers can and do choose what, when and where to read

Being a discriminating reader often involves knowing what you don't want to read. This session raises some of the 'rights of a reader' (Pennac, 1994).

Before the session:
Invite the teachers to bring some reading they have either not enjoyed or have chosen not to finish. Session leaders should also bring some of their own.

During the session:
Share these texts and list their reasons for reading them on a flip chart. What do these reveal about readers and reading?

Make a 'book blanket' with the group, spreading out all available texts and magazines, non fiction and poetry over several tables and then examining this book spread. Ask the teachers to find one book they would not want to read and discuss why. Are they influenced by the cover, the author, the blurb, the subject matter? Also ask them to find a book they would like to read and again reflect upon the reasons given.

Share Pennac's The Rights of a Reader with the group:

> ### The Rights of a Reader
> 1. The right not to read
> 2. The right to skip pages
> 3. The right not to finish a book
> 4. The right to re-read
> 5. The right to read anything
> 6. The right to 'bovarysme (a textually transmissible disease)
> 7. The right to browse
> 8. The right to read out loud
> 9. The right to remain silent.
> (Pennac, 1994: 145-6)

(This was first developed in Pennac's 1994 book but is available from Walker books as a poster illustrated by Quentin Blake.)

Discuss with the teachers whether the children in their classes have such rights. What is the role of choice and agency in reading? How would they feel if they lost their rights as readers? What are the implications for classroom practice?

If teachers discuss Pennac's nine rights with their classes, this might lead to establishing more comfortable reading corners or the freedom to sit where they wish in ERIC time, and /or photographic displays of children, staff, parents and family members reading in their favourite places at home. (See also session for Aim 2a p 21). Additionally, displays of texts which children did not finish, with brief commentaries about why they decided not to continue, can be created to demonstrate the rights of all readers to exercise choice and agency.

> *I did not finish Megastar Mysteries because it got boring, as I did not understand some of the words and I did not know what was happening in the story.* (Eva, aged 8)

6 Recommended Reading and Websites

Bromley, H. (2002) Meet the Simpsons. *The Primary English Magazine* 7(4): 7–11 http://www.garthpublishing.co.uk/pem.php

Cremin, T., Bearne, E., Mottram, M. and Goodwin, P. (2007) *Teachers as Readers* Phase 1 (2006-7) Research Report http://www.ukla.org/downloads/TARwebreport.doc

Cremin, T. (2007) Revisiting reading for pleasure: diversity, delight and desire. in K. Goouch and A. Lambirth (eds) *Teaching Reading, Teaching Phonics: Critical Perspectives*. Milton Keynes: Open University.

Cremin, T., Bearne, E., Goodwin, P. and Mottram, M. (2008a) Primary Teachers as Readers. *English in Education*, 42 (1): 8-23

Cremin, T., Mottram, M. Bearne, E., Goodwin, P. (2008b) Exploring teachers' knowledge of children's literature. *The Cambridge Journal of Education*, 38 (4)

Goodwin, P. (ed.) (2008) *Understanding Children's Books: a guide for education professionals*. London: SAGE.

Lockwood, M. (2008) *Reading for Purpose and Pleasure in the Primary School*. London: SAGE.

Martin, T. (2003) Minimum and maximum entitlements: literature at Key Stage 2, *Reading, Literacy and Language*, 37(1):14–18

Moss, G.(2007) *Literacy and Gender: researching texts, contents and readers*. London: Routledge.

For more details about action research see: Bearne, E., Graham, L., Marsh, J. (2007) *Classroom Action Research in Literacy: a guide to practice*. Leicester: UKLA.

Websites

United Kingdom Literacy Association (UKLA) http://www.ukla.org

Primary National Strategy (PNS) http://www.standards.dfes.gov.uk/primaryframework

National Literacy Trust (NLT) http://www.literacytrust.org.uk/

Progress in International Literacy Study Report on England (PIRLS)
http://www.nfer.ac.uk/publications/other-publications/downloadable-reports/pirls-2006.cfm

The Reading Agency (RA) Summer Reading Challenge
http://www.readingagency.org.uk/children/summer-reading-challenge/

The Reader Organisation http://www.getintoreading.org/

Book review and literature websites

Write Away http://www.writeaway.org.uk/

Books for Keeps http://www.booksfor keeps.co.uk

Children's Poetry Archive http://www.poetryarchive.org/childrensarchive/home.do

Book Trust Children's Books http://www.booktrustchildrensbooks.org.uk/

Reading Zone http://www.readingzone.com/

This section contains material to support data gathering at the start and end of the project. There are also proformas to help teachers to record the impact of their work on their focus pupils and on their own professional learning.

You may want to give the following list to the teachers to support them collecting project information.

As a teacher you need to carry out the following at the beginning of the project:

- consider ethical issues
- discuss with your headteacher the school policy for seeking parental permission to photograph, video or audiotape children
- seek written permission from parents to use their children's voices, images, writing or drawing (A5)
- identify three case-study children
- plan a school development project related to two or more of the aims.

You will need to collect the following data for your portfolio:

Autumn Term: Getting Started and Planning

- Children's Reading Survey (A1) for each of your 3 Case Study children. (You may wish to carry this out with your class.)
- Children's Reading Profiles (A2) for your Case Study children.
- Termly Observations of Case Study Children (A3)
- *Teachers as Readers* Questionnaire (B1)
- Personal Reading History (B2)
- Termly Reflections on Being a Reading Teacher (B3)
- Additional Child Information (A4) and Additional Teacher Information (B5)
- Termly Reflections on Impact (B4)

Spring Term: Implementing the Plan

- Termly Observations of Case Study Children (A3)
- Additional Child Information (A4) and Additional Teacher Information (B5)
- Termly Reflections on being a Reading Teacher (B3)
- Termly Reflections on Impact (B4)

Summer Term: Continued Implementation and Examining Outcomes: reflection, analysis and evaluation

- Children's Reading Survey (A1) for the three Case Study children.
- Children Reading Profiles (A2) for your Case Study children.
- Termly Observations of Case Study Children (A3)
- *Teachers as Readers* Questionnaire (B1)
- Termly Reflections on Being a Reading Teacher sheet (B3)
- Additional Child Information (A4) and Additional Teacher Information (B5)
- Termly Reflections on Impact sheet (B4)
- Presentation of Findings (B6)
- Final Project Evaluation (B7)

1. Tick one box:

I love reading   It's okay   I am not bothered   I don't like reading

☐   ☐   ☐   ☐

2. Tick one box:

I'm a very   I'm a   I'm okay   I'm not very good
good reader   good reader

☐   ☐   ☐   ☐

3. Do you read more at home or at school? _____

Why do you think this is? _____

_____

4. Do you read with anyone at home?

Yes   No

☐   ☐

Who do you read with? _____

What sorts of things? _____

_____

5. Which two of these do you enjoy reading most? Please tick your 2 favourites.

Joke   Magazines   Comics   Fiction   TV guides   Poetry
                                                            /mags

☐   ☐   ☐   ☐   ☐   ☐

6. What are you reading in school? _____

7. Who is your favourite author? _____

8. What's your favourite book ever? _____

9. Do you ever talk about what you're reading? Please tick all that apply

With friends	With mum	With dad	With grandparents	With sisters/brothers
☐	☐	☐	☐	☐

Anyone else? _____

10. Do you think your teacher reads?

Definitely	Probably	Probably not	Definitely not
☐	☐	☐	☐

11. Does your teacher?

Love reading	Think it's okay	Is not bothered	Doesn't like it
☐	☐	☐	☐

12. Does your teacher read aloud?

Every day	Several times a week	Once a week	Less than once a week
☐	☐	☐	☐

Name _____ Teacher's name _____

Year Group _____ Date _____ School _____

Thank you

A2 Children's Reading Profiles

Child's Name _____ **Age** _____ **Year Group** _____

Teacher's name _____ **School** _____

Please comment on the child's attitudes and behaviours as well as knowledge and skill.

Please comment on your knowledge of the child as a reader in a range of classroom contexts.

Please provide any information you may have about the child's reading habits outside school.

Please provide a profile of the child as a reader from both test and classroom contexts.

Best fit N.C. Level   Evidence drawn upon (e.g. APP or other assessment tool)

Child's Name _____ **Age** _____ **Year Group** _____

Teacher's name _____ **LA** _____

Observations: what to look out for

Reading strategies: developing a range of strategies or dependent on one or two?

Confidence: view of self as reader	Pleasure and enjoyment	Independence
Stamina: reading at length; tackling challenging texts	Developing experience as a reader; choosing books, preferences	Favourite books or authors
Talking about reading	Reading at home	Reading with friends and family
Interpreting and responding to images, own drawings	Relating reading to own experiences and culture	Writing about reading
Writing in role	Reflecting on reading, articulating understanding	

Observations: Where? When?

1:1 conversations	1:1 reading	guided group	whole class
conversations with parents, siblings	literacy work	library	reading diaries
reading aloud	silent reading		

You may want to include additional information in your portfolio about each of your Case Study children or about any changing patterns in attitudes to reading or achievement of the class as a whole.

These might include:

- additional observations of Case Study children in a range of contexts
- annotated photocopies of the Case Study children's reading records to show development
- annotated photocopies of the Case Study children's home-school books to show development
- Assessing Pupil Progress (APP) records across the year
- annotated samples of children's writing in response to reading
- notes about significant conversations with children about their reading
- transcripts of conversations or notes on reading conferences
- photographs of children engaged in reading activities or events over the period of the project
- photographs of Case Study children involved in reading activities
- photographs of project related events with a brief explanatory sentence or two photographs taken by the children themselves of reading activities they engage in, inside or outside school.

You may also want to keep a learning journal or research diary to record valuable information about children's reading behaviours and habits across the curriculum and out of school.

A5 Parent/Carer Consent Guidance

Teachers only need to gain parental consent if they are going to undertake activities involving children beyond what is normal practice in their school. It is good practice for information to be shared with parents and colleagues about the project and for consent to be sought for such things as photographs. The process of reflecting on the research helps to focus the design around respect for participants and child protection issues. Teachers could usefully therefore:

- provide information about the reasons why they are doing the research
- explain the research activities and the ways in which the children will be involved
- explain whether these things will happen inside/outside the normal school curriculum
- inform parents/carers about anything that constitutes practice that is different from the norm
- inform them how data will be stored, whether it will be confidential or whether it will be shared and with whom
- ask parents/carers to discuss the project with their child
- explain what will happen to the data/evidence in the long run
- explain how and when will they will inform people about their findings.

If teachers feel there are aspects of the research for which they need parental consent, then they can offer a series of statements for parents to opt into or out of, making it clear that parents can change their minds at any time without needing to give a reason. In any letter to parents/carers it is helpful to offer them an informative paragraph about the work first and then the following could be used:

Please tick the boxes as applicable

I have read and understood the Name of Project **information for parents / carers.**

☐ **Yes** ☐ **No**

I consent to Name of researcher **taking photographs of my child for research purposes.**

☐ **Yes** ☐ **No**

I consent to the photographs being used in presentations and publications for educational purposes.

☐ **Yes** ☐ **No**

Name of child _____   Signature of parent /carer _____

Date _____   Relationship to child _____

Ensure that there is a contact name and number in case parents want to ask any questions.

B1 *Teachers as Readers* Questionnaire

Name: _____ **School:** _____

Year Group you Teach: _____ **Years in Teaching:** _____ **Date:** _____

1. What have you read recently for your own pleasure? _____

_____

When did you read this?:   **Within the last month**   **Within the last 3 months**

Circle or underline   **Within the last 6 months**   **Over 6 months ago**

2. List 6 children's book authors

_____
_____
_____
_____
_____
_____

3. List 6 children's poets

_____
_____
_____
_____
_____
_____

4. List 6 children's picture book authors/illustrators

_____
_____
_____
_____
_____
_____

5. Please rate your subject knowledge about children's literature *(from 6 for 'highly knowledgeable' to 1 'limited knowledge', circling your choice)*

6   **5**   **4**   **3**   **2**   **1**

Please comment on this: do you, for example, feel more knowledgeable about particular genres/ poets/authors? _____

_____
_____
_____
_____
_____

6. In what ways do you use your knowledge of children's literature in developing children as readers? _____

_____
_____
_____
_____
_____

7. Which of the following is the most influential in helping you decide which children's books to use in class? (Please number from 5 most influential to 1 least influential)

☐ Personal interest/knowledge ☐ Children's recommendations ☐ Library service

☐ Literacy co-ordinators' recommendations ☐ Other

8. In the last year, have you involved ☐ **parents?** ☐ **librarians?** (please tick)

Please give details _____
_____
_____
_____
_____
_____

9. Do you use publishers' prepared materials in teaching literacy? (please circle)

Daily　　　　**Weekly**　　　　**Monthly**　　　　**Infrequently**

If so, what do you use them for? _____
_____
_____
_____
_____

10. Rank the following statements in descending order of importance (5 is most important)

Literature is important because it...

☐ **develops reading**

☐ **develops writing**

☐ **widens knowledge**

☐ **engages the emotions**

☐ **develops the imagination**

Personal Reading History		
Texts	**Significant People / Places**	**Talk**
Note all the kinds of reading you remember from when you were young: books, comics, magazines, newspapers, letters diaries, screen reading, maps, holy texts, songs, cereal boxes…	Was anyone involved in this reading with you? Where did you usually read?	What kinds of talk and conversations were involved?

42

A Reading Teacher: a teacher who reads and a reader who teaches (Commeyras *et al.*, 2003).

Name _____ **School** _____ **Date** _____

1. **What have you read recently - children's and/or adult texts - that has been memorable and/or valuable to you?**
   Please name the authors and the books and explain why their book(s) have been memorable or valuable to you.

2. **What have you learnt about/do you know about yourself as a reader?**
   For example, about your reading history, current habits, preference, practices, places you choose to read, people who you talk to about what you are reading...

3. What links have you made in the classroom explicitly to the children about your own reading: the content of what you read, your views and responses to what you are reading, your habits as a reader of different texts, how you engage with the reading process and so on.
Please be both general and specific and describe at least one example when you have shared something of yourself as a reader and how the children and you responded.

4. What are your plans for making more explicit Reading Teacher links with the children in your class and in the school?
Again please be specific; this is a new challenge and will not just happen unless it is planned and integrated into your practice.

B4 Termly Reflections on Impact

Name _____ **School** _____ **Date** _____

1. Actions: What changes have you made to your practice when developing children's independent reading for pleasure (in teaching, text provision, text recommendations, time and opportunity, making new links with parents, librarians and so on)?

2. Impact: What impact is evident in the case study children's engagement, attitudes and strategies?

3. Evidence: How do you know the work has impacted on the children? What is your evidence? Try to refer to accompanying materials, label these and place them in your portfolio.

4. Reflections: In what ways is your thinking about reading and teaching reading changing?

You may want to include additional information in your portfolio relevant to your own professional learning to help document your journey towards the class or whole school aims for the project, bearing in mind the four overarching project aims:

1. Widen teachers' knowledge of children's literature in order to support independent reading for pleasure.
2. Develop teachers' confidence and skilful use of such literature in the classroom in order to foster reading for pleasure.
3. Develop teachers' relationships with parents, carers, librarians and families in order to support independent reading for pleasure.
4. Enable teachers to understand the value of becoming a Reading Teacher: a teacher who reads and a reader who teaches in order to support independent reading for pleasure.

For example, you may wish to include some of the following:

- the school/class *Building Communities of Readers* Action Plan and documentary evidence of change (Figure 3)
- lists of children's/ adult books recently read
- planning sheets and commentaries noting and evaluating the use of new strategies
- medium term plans which reflect new ways of working
- new school policy documents developed from the project
- notes and plans of staff /governors' meetings focused on Building Communities of Readers
- research journals documenting your action research and comments on the focus children
- reading logs with comments on your own reading, your habits and practices
- children's work triggered by new ways of working
- notes and photographs from meetings/ initiatives libraries
- details of new links or activities developed with families, parents.

The research and development project *Building Communities of Readers* aimed to develop children's independent pleasure in reading by:

1. Widening teachers' knowledge of children's literature in order to support independent reading for pleasure.

2. Developing teachers' confidence and skilful use of such literature in the classroom in order to foster reading for pleasure.

3. Developing teachers' relationships with parents, carers, librarians and families, in order to support independent reading for pleasure.

4. Helping teachers understand the value of becoming a Reading Teacher: a teacher who reads and a reader who teaches in order to support independent reading for pleasure.

In your school you may have set your own aims in relation to developing children's independent reading for pleasure, so in your project presentation it is suggested you might seek to encompass the following key issues.

1. AIMS
Given the project aims above, what aims did you choose to focus on in your school action plan and why?

2. CONTEXT
Offer a short description of your school and previous practice/ knowledge in your chosen area.

3. ACTIVITIES
What practical activities have you introduced in order to increase children's pleasure and independence as readers? (Depending on your role, this might be in your classroom, across the school or a mixture of both.)

4. IMPACT
What difference have the changes made to the children? You may want to talk here about your three focus children, or focus on just one of them and relate this to the impact on the class. What difference have the changes made to the staff and school as a whole?

5. EVIDENCE
How do you know your work has had an impact? What is your evidence? Try to share the children's voices (e.g. observations, photographs, transcripts, samples of work, drawings) and analyse the evidence as proof of impact. Also make use of staff voices and evidence of their changed practice.

6. IMPLICATIONS FOR FUTURE WORK
What will you do now to continue the learning journey for: the children; yourself; the school; parent/community/library partnerships?

B7 Final Project Evaluation

Name _____ **School** _____ **Date** _____

1. What impact has this project had upon your **knowledge of children's literature** and other texts? *Have you widened your repertoire of texts - if so in what ways?*

2. What impact has this project had upon your **pedagogy**? *Has an increase in subject knowledge led to different classroom practices, such as text recommendations, ERIC time, reading corners, unit planning, reading aloud and so on?*

3. What impact has any change you have experienced in your knowledge and pedagogy had on the **children in your class**? *Please be as specific as possible with regard to named case study children and others.*

4. What impact has the project had upon other **members of staff** in your school? *What evidence do you have?*

5. What specific changes in policy or practice have been implemented **across the whole school** to support all the children's pleasure and development as independent readers?

. In what ways has the project work led to **new partnerships/communities** with parents, carers and others such as librarians?

. What impact has being a **Reading Teacher**, (a teacher who reads and a reader who teaches) and who talks about their reading habits and preferences and encourages the children to do likewise, had upon you and the children?

. What would you say have been the **most significant positive outcomes** of this project for:
(a) you
(b) children in your class
(c) your school as a whole?

. What are your **future targets** emerging from this project?

0. Any other comments or thoughts?

hank you for your commitment, energy and involvement throughout the project.

References

Arts Council England (2003) *From Looking Glass to Spy Glass: a consultation paper on children's literature*. London: Arts Council.

Arizpe, E. and Styles, M. (2003) *Children Reading Pictures: Interpreting Visual Texts*. London: Routledge Falmer.

Barrs, M. and Cork, V. (2001) *The Reader in the Writer: The Influence of Literature upon Writing at KS2*. London: Centre for Literacy in Primary Education.

Bearne, E. (2003) Playing with possibilities: children's multidimensional texts, in E. Bearne, H. Dombey and T. Grainger (eds) Classroom Interactions in Literacy. Maidenhead: Open University Press.

Bearne, E., Clark, C., Johnson, A., Manford, P., Mottram, M., Wolstencroft, H. (2007) *Reading on Screen*. Leicester: United Kingdom Literacy Association.

BERA (2004) *Revised Ethical Guidelines for Educational Research*. Nottingham: British Educational Research Association.

Bisplinghoff, B.S. (2003) Teachers'planning as responsible resistance. *Language Arts* 80 (3): 119-128

Block, C., Oakar, M., and Hurt, N. (2002) The expertise of literacy teachers: A continuum from preschool to Grade 5. *Reading Research Quarterly* 37(2):178-206

Britton, J. (1993) *Literature in its Place*. Portsmouth, NH: Boynton/Cook/Heinemann.

Bromley, H. (2000) 'Never be without a Beano': Comics, children and literacy, in H. Anderson and M. Styles *Teaching Through Texts*. London, Routledge.

Chambers, A. (1995) Book Talk: *Occasional Writing on Literature and Children*. Stroud, Glos.: The Thimble Press

Clark, C. and Foster, A. (2005) *Children's and young people's reading habits and preferences: the who,what, why, where and when*. London: National Literacy Trust.

Commeyras, M., Bisplinghoff, B.S. and Olson, J. (2003) *Teachers as Readers: perspectives on the importance of reading in teachers' classrooms and lives*. Newark: International Reading Association.

Cremin, T. (2007) Revisiting reading for pleasure: diversity, delight and desire in K. Goouch and A. Lambirth (eds) *Teaching Reading, Teaching Phonics: Critical Perspectives*. Milton Keynes: Open University Press.

Cremin, T., Bearne, E., Mottram, M. and Goodwin, P. (2007) *Teachers as Readers* Phase 1 (2006-7) Research Report. http://www.ukla.org/downloads/TARwebreport.doc

Cremin, T., Bearne, E., Goodwin, P. and Mottram, M. (2008a) Primary Teachers as Readers. *English in Education* 42 (1): 8-23

Cremin, T., Mottram, M. Bearne, E., Goodwin, P. (2008b) Exploring teachers' knowledge of children's literature. *The Cambridge Journal of Education* 38 (4).

Cremin, T., Mottram, M., Collins, F. and Powell, S. (2008c) *Teachers as Readers: Building Communities of Readers. Report to the Esmée Fairbairn Foundation*. London, Esmée Fairbairn Foundation.

Dombey, H. (1998) Changing literacy in the early years of school, in B. Cox (ed) *Literacy is not Enough*. Manchester: Manchester University Press and Book Trust.

Dreher, M. (2003) Motivating teachers to read. *The Reading Teacher*, 56(4): 338–40

Durrant, J. (2008) *Evaluation of Teachers as Readers: Building Communities of Readers*. Report for the Esmée Fairbairn Foundation.

Frater, G. (2000) Observed in practice, English in the National Literacy Strategy: some reflections. *Reading* 34(3):107–12

Gonzalez, N., and Moll, L. (2002) *Funds of Knowledge: Theorizing Practices in Households, Communities, and Classrooms*. New Jersey: Lawrence Erlbaum Associates.

Hitchcock, G. and Hughes, D. (1995) *Research and the Teacher* (2nd edition). London: Routledge Falmer.

Hurd, S., Dixon, M. and Oldham, J. (2006) Are low levels of book spending in primary schools jeopardising the National Literacy Strategy? *The Curriculum Journal* 17(1): 73-88

King, C. (2001) "I like group reading because we can share ideas" - the role of talk within the literature circle. *Reading, Literacy and Language* 35(1): 32–6

Martin,T. (2003) Minimum and maximum entitlements: literature at key stage 2. *Reading Literacy and Language* 37(1):14-17

Maybin, J. and Moss, G. (1993) Talk about Texts: reading as a social event. *Journal of Research in Reading* 16(2):138-147

Maynard, S. Mackay, S. Smyth, F and Reynolds, K. (2007) *Young People's Reading in 2005: the second study of young people's reading habits.* Loughborough and Roehampton: USU and NCRCL

McCarthey, S.J. and Moje, E.B (2002) Identity Matters. *Reading Research Quarterly* 37(2): 228-238

McNiff, J., Lomax, P. and Whitehead, J. (2nd edition) (2003) *You and Your Action Research Project.* London: Routledge Falmer.

Medwell, J., Wray, D., Poulson, L. and Fox, R. (1998) *Effective Teachers of Literacy: A Report of a Research Project Commissioned by the Teacher Training Agency.* Exeter: University of Exeter.

Morrison, T., Jacobs, J. Swinyard, W. (1999) Do teachers who read personally use recommended literacy practices in their classrooms? *Reading Research and Instruction* 38(2): 81-100

Mullis, I.V.S., Martin, M.O., Gonzalez, E.J. and Kennedy, A.M. (2003) *PIRLS 2001 International Report:* IEA's Study of Reading Literacy Achievement in Primary Schools. Chestnut Hill, MA: Boston College.

Nestle Family Monitor (2003) Number 17, November http://www.literacytrust.org.uk/ (accessed 3rd August, 2008).

OECD-PISA (2001) *Knowledge and Skills for Life. First results from PISA 2000.* Paris: OECD Publications

Office for Standards in Education OfSTED (2004a) *Reading for Purpose and Pleasure: An Evaluation of the Teaching of Reading in Primary School*, London: OfSTED.

Office for Standards in Education (OfSTED) (2004b) Conference Report by Phil Jarrett, OfSTED, Subject Conference July 2004.

Office for Standards in Education (OfSTED) (2007) *Poetry in Schools: a survey of Practice 2006/7.* London: OfSTED December, 2007.

Pennac, D.(1994) *Reads Like a Novel.* London: Quartet Books.

Powling, C., Ashley, B., Pullman, P., Fine, A. and Gavin, J. (eds) (2003) *Meetings with the Minister.* Reading: National Centre for Language and Literacy.

Powling, C., Ashley, B., Pullman, P., Fine, A. and Gavin, J. (2005) *Beyond Bog Standard Literacy.* Reading: National Centre for Language and Literacy.

Sainsbury, M. and Schagen, I. (2004) Attitudes to reading at ages nine and eleven *Journal of Research in Reading* 27(3): 373-386

Sedgwick, F. (2001) *Teaching Literacy: A Creative Approach.* London: Continuum.

Spufford, F. (2002) *The Child that Books Built.* London: Faber and Faber.

Training and Development Agency for Schools (2007) Professional Standards for Teachers http://www.tda.gov.uk/teachers/ professionalstandards.aspx

Twist, L., Schagen, I. and Hodgson, C. (2003) *Readers and Reading: the National Report for England (PIRLS).* Slough: NFER.

Twist, L., Schagen, I. and Hodgson, C. (2007) *Readers and Reading: the National Report for England (PIRLS).* Slough NFER.

Washtell, A. (2008) Getting to Grips with Phonics in J. Graham & A. Kelly, (eds) *Reading under Control*, London: David Fulton (first published 1997)

IDEAS IN PRACTICE 2

Planning for Literacy
Helen Wolstencroft

One of the recurring issues in primary classrooms at present is the lack of confidence some teachers experience when required to plan a unit of work for their class from scratch. Based on the planning phases model used in the Primary Framework, this booklet makes successful planning practices explicit and provides support for shared dialogue between colleagues in schools and Local Authorities. With illustrated formats, each phase of the model is examined to show how planning can scaffold learning and the materials give suggestions about adapting planning to meet pedagogic, personal and professional needs. Particular attention is given to the integration of the phonic, spelling and sentence strands of the Primary Framework and the place of guided sessions within a unit.

UKLA's FIRST CDROM RESOURCE

Guided Reading using Short Texts at KS2
Pam Dowson, Kerry Henderson, Emma Poole, Sarah Thrower and Sally Wilkinson
edited by Eve Bearne

Created in collaboration with Suffolk Local Authority, this CDROM has been put together to help answer teachers' concerns about how to manage Guided Reading at Key Stage 2. The materials, with examples all developed by teachers, offer advice on how to choose texts to improve children's reading skills while genuinely engaging a group of young readers over an extended period of time. The suggestions and examples use short texts as a way of getting to higher level discussion quickly, helping children to respond critically.

The materials include a generic teaching sequence for working with a text over a period of several weeks with case study examples and teaching sequences for years 3,4 5 and 6 using:

- short stories and short novels • complex picturebooks
- information texts including the internet • poetry and song.

Each case study and teaching sequence gives examples of questions aimed at specific Assessment Focuses.

There are sections giving advice on managing groups, asking questions, working with Teaching Assistants and developing independent activities. The section on recording and assessing progress provides a detailed grid developed by Suffolk LA for making judgements and links with the recent developments in Assessing Pupil Progress.

To order, contact:

UKLA, 4th Floor, Attenborough Building, University of Leicester, Leicester LE1 7RH
Tel: 0116 229 7450   Fax: 0116 229 7451   Email: admin@ukla.org

Or visit our online bookshop at www.ukla.org